GERRY CAMBRIDGE WAS BORN OF IRISH parents in 1
he worked as a freelance natural history photographer
numerous publications including *Reader's Digest, BBC*
magazines of the RSPCA, and the photographic press. For 25 years he
lived in a caravan in rural Ayrshire. In 1995 he founded, and still edits,
The Dark Horse, Scotland's foremost poetry magazine, international in
scope, with strong links to America and a particular interest in poetry
in metre and rhyme. As the Brownsbank Writing Fellow for 1997–99,
based at Hugh MacDiarmid's former home near Biggar, South Lanarkshire,
he has worked frequently in primary and secondary schools, and with
writers' groups, giving mixed-media presentations involving nature poetry,
photographs, and blues harmonica. *'Nothing But Heather!'* is his second
book of verse.

By the same Author:

The Shell House 1995 (Scottish Cultural Press)
The Dark Gift & other Poems 1996 (St. Inan's Press)

'Nothing but Heather!'

Scottish Nature in Poems, Photographs and Prose

GERRY CAMBRIDGE

Luath Press Limited
EDINBURGH
www.luath.co.uk

First Edition 1999

The paper used in this book is recyclable.
It is produced in a low energy, low emission manner
from renewable forests.

Printed and bound by MFP Design & Print, Manchester.

Colour origination by The Quick Brown Fox Company (Scotland) Ltd.

Designed by Tom Bee

Typeset in Sabon

The publisher acknowledges subsidy from

THE SCOTTISH ARTS COUNCIL

towards the publication of this volume

For Jim and Matt Bain
Sam Gilliland
and my nieces and nephews:
Siobhan, Lisa, Kieran and Declan,
in the hope that their world be
full of species

Acknowledgements

MY THANKS are due to Carcanet Press for permission to quote from *The Complete Poems* of Hugh MacDiarmid; to Jim and Janet Wiltshire, and to James Brockway, for assistance in preparing this project; to the Scottish Arts Council and the Brownsbank Committee, especially Jenny Brown, Gavin Wallace, Jim Ness, Bill Deerin, Ann Matheson and Edith Ryan; and greatest thanks to Aileen McIntyre, first and best reader and critic of the poems and prose.

Technical note about the photographs

MOST OF THESE pictures were shot on Kodachrome 25 and 64 colour transparency film on a Nikon F2A with a 55mm Micro-nikkor or a Vivitar 135mm close-focus lens, occasionally with extension tubes or other more makeshift arrangements.

The remainder of the photographs were taken on a Bronica ECII medium-format camera with an 80mm Zenzanon lens, on Ektachrome 64 colour transparency film.

Where possible, natural light was used, but for some of the more specialist shots up to 3 flash heads were required.

Contents

Words Through the Lens

An Introduction

> Scotland small? Our multiform, our infinite Scotland *small*?
> Only as a patch of hillside may be a cliché corner
> To a fool who cries 'Nothing but Heather!'...

HUGH MACDIARMID'S POEM, printed as 'Scotland Small?' in anthologies, appears in his *Complete Poems* as part of the long work 'Direadh I'. As well as expressing withering scorn towards, in all likelihood, a complacent Englishman, 'Scotland Small?' goes on to catalogue in rebuttal a modest range of Scottish natural history, a number of species of which feature in this book. Brownsbank Cottage, in which I write this, and where MacDiarmid lived for the last 27 years of his life from 1951 to 1978, was an appropriate setting for a writer whose imagination was watermarked with country life and happenings. The cottage sits at around 700 feet above sea-level, among the feminine lines of the Border Hills, some three miles north-east of Biggar in South Lanarkshire, up a farm track. It is the only A-grade listed farm cottage in Scotland, on account of its association with the poet, as well as a registered museum and the home, usually for two-year periods, of a visiting writer.

It is difficult to get far from nature here, indoors as well as out. Woodmice move in in the winter, and their arrival can be definite: on the first frosty night last December, suddenly they were here. One could almost have imagined them, from the frozen woods, saying "Time to hit the Penthouse Suite!", then packing their bags and arriving *en masse*. I call the low wood-panelled ceiling in MacDiarmid's room 'the mice's ballroom', from their habit of performing dances in the loft above, perhaps to the music that is the warmth from the coal fire. I have no problem agreeing that, as Walt Whitman wrote, "A mouse is sufficient to stagger sextillions of infidels." How far must you take a mouse from its place of capture for it not to find its way back home? One mile. Last winter I observed one such release by my neighbour, Dave Cooper. In the faint glow of the street light, he removed the lid from the biscuit tin which contained the infidel-staggerer. Nothing but chewed-up bits of paper could at first be seen. Then, suddenly, at the corner of the tin, a head appeared, fine-snouted, brilliant-eyed, whiskers quivering, ears poised — a picture of absolute wild vivacity, as if the energy that lighted a town had been concentrated in this tiny creature. For an instant we stared at each other, face to face, mouse and I. Then it simply leapt out of the tin into space, describing a parabola, and was away into the darkness as soon as it touched the ground.

As well as home to mice, Brownsbank is an arachnologist's dream, and slugs of all shapes and sizes glide serenely under the door and may be found in the kitchen and bathroom, their eye stalks extended, sailing like miniscule silent liners the oceans of the formica and enamel surfaces. Velvet ground beetles, nearly an inch long, are also common additions to the Brownsbank Bestiary; black, with a sheen of sacerdotal purple, they are predator-scavengers with secateur jaws and appear from under the bed to prowl the savannah of the floor until stopped by an imposing foot. Then they turn tail and scuttle off, in panic. And the cottage has the usual collection of forkietails and slaters, the latter appearing to climb up out of the drainpipe in the bath, to sit motionless on the white enamel until, queerly purposeless, they die.

Nature, of course, is more prevalent outside. The fields and hedges round about are hoaching with rabbits. White scuts flash away in dozens round every corner. Buzzards orbit above the hills with long "peeooo" cries. On spring nights last year, returning in the dark to Brownsbank, before I rattled the key in the lock (imagining the house's spirits fleeing before me) I'd stand and listen to peewits and snipe going mad with spring exuberance in the marsh below the cottage. In July, the woods and slopes are lavish with foxglove spires, both red and white, in breeze-quivered hundreds. Last summer, an oystercatcher in the meadow at the bottom of the brae, at Candymill, instead of nesting on the ground as usual, opted to use a broad stob in a fence. It laid its three eggs in the hollow top, on wood chippings. There it sat, incongruous but admirable, four feet above its fellows. An individualist. Perhaps it is a new subspecies, *Haemotopus ostralegus MacDiarmidus*.

Further afield, the number of kills on the roads of rural South Lanarkshire attest to the health of the fauna — badgers, foxes, hedgehogs. One day in October 1997, riding by motorbike to Glasgow, I passed a freshly-killed Barn Owl on the Biggar to Lanark road. It was still warm. Its eyes were still open. Its feathers were unruffled and immaculate. Not able to bear leaving it on the road, with no clear intent I wrapped it up carefully in polythene bags and put it in my rucksack. The following day I buried the bird under the cherry tree in Brownsbank's garden, and wrote this:

Talisman

Struck by a speeding car,
the barn owl, found at the road-edge,
which half an hour before
had quartered the fields and sedge
of October Lanarkshire
now lies with a foot of earth
added to the air
between it and the Pole Star,
in Brownsbank's garden.
With a spade I set it in —
pure white, and airy gold
diamonded with charcoal,
its heart-shaped face not sad
but breathtaking,
its active warmth now cold,
for earth's process to begin.

Like an image of the soul
or what the soul might be,
its incorruptibility
that had flown in the crisp night
about the starlit fields
of this landlocked county,
now under the cherry tree
in Brownsbank's garden set;
through the nights of hail and sleet
and the lashing windy wet
I have it to remind me
as talisman yet.

The poem and the ritual it describes were the establishing of Brownsbank as a place to write, for myself.

For inhabiting a museum devoted to a famous dead writer, as a living writer, is a delicate business. "I start to fit my day between the portraits, books, his pipes..." wrote James Robertson, the first Brownsbank Fellow, in his powerful poem 'The Blues at Brownsbank.' "[I] sleep every nicht/ wi the deid", my predecessor Matthew Fitt wrote, in his poem 'Fellow'. Brownsbank is crowded with memorabilia devoted to MacDiarmid and his wife, Valda: over a dozen portraits on the wall in his room stare down incessantly. No writer can afford to let another dictate to him or her an aesthetic, and MacDiarmid was often prescriptive in his pronouncements. As with Burns, he is an example of a great poet who could exert a negative influence on other writers. His near-contemporary, W. S. Graham, left Scotland at least partly in reaction to the Scottish Renaissance led by MacDiarmid. Some younger writers get round the problem of MacDiarmid's presence either by ignoring him or by iconoclasm: to Kathleen Jamie as a young woman, "MacDiarmid seemed," as she wrote in *Poetry Review* in 1997, "a ridiculous cockerel, crowing on his tartan midden." Yet to poet and academic Alan Riach, editor of Carcanet's *MacDiarmid 2,000* project, which aims to have the Collected MacDiarmid in print by the millennium, MacDiarmid "was the most important thing to happen in Scotland since 1707," as he wrote in a letter published in *The Herald* of June 5, 1995. One feels one should make allowance for his academic bias. Douglas Dunn, in his multi-faceted and courageous essay 'Hugh MacDiarmid: Inhuman Splendours', in the *New Edinburgh Review* in 1980, castigated what he saw as the indiscriminate tendency towards hagiography among a number of contributors to the essay collection, *The Age of MacDiarmid.*

Nature makes frequent appearances in MacDiarmid's poems. One long poem dedicated to William Soutar, 'Tam O' The Wilds and the Many-faced Mystery' is an account of Tam, an amateur naturalist of the old type, in the era before all knowledge had to be certificated to be deemed authentic. Tam is autodidact, fanatical, and knowledgeable: "First hand knowledge was what he aye prized,/ And personal observation was his constant pride," MacDiarmid writes, approvingly. In another MacDiarmid poem, 'Dytiscus', the narrator compares himself to that creature. *Dytiscus marginalis,* the Great Diving Beetle, is a savage predator in ponds, both as larva and adult. The larva grows to around two inches in length. It is basically a stomach attached to two curved hypodermics. The latter it uses to stab prey, then suck out its bodily juices. The adult beetle is similarly ferocious. Some one and a half inches long, worthy of Breughel's imagination, the creature will attack one's finger if it's suspected of being edible. The narrator in MacDiarmid's poem asks "Must men to higher things ascend / For air like the Dytiscus there...", before likening himself to "A water beetle of the brain." It is a bold analogy to anyone who has seen *Dytiscus* at work in an aquarium.

MacDiarmid's mental robustness and his plain fascination in the face of nature is an exhilarating world away from Housman's cry of "heartless, witless nature!", or of Tennyson's dread and depression at the implications of Darwinism. Where a weasel hunting among tree roots might have been occasion, one imagines, for a lamentation on Tennyson's part, MacDiarmid uses it, in a lyric in Scots, for a striking comparison: "As a futret bobbin in a bourachie o scrogs/Is the glory o God i the hearts o men." There is something meliorist about MacDiarmid's imagination. In a sense, he uses nature to make metaphorical leaps applicable to humanity, certainly in the last two poems quoted.

It is interesting to compare such MacDiarmid poems which feature nature with those of another Scottish poet who was often drawn to similar subject matter. Norman MacCaig was one of MacDiarmid's closest friends (MacCaig's wife owned the cottage 200 yards down the brae from Brownsbank, within convenient post-whisky walking distance). MacCaig called himself, jocularly, a 'zen calvinist', but there seems more than a little truth in the phrase. His poems on birds and other natural history, when they don't degenerate into a sort of poetical burlesque, have a zen-like radiance, an observation purely of the moment which is surely a form of grace — a word he didn't accept. So he ends his poem 'Starling': "Now he's flown up like a mad glove onto a fence post./He squinnies at the world and draws a cork from a bottle."

The image of the glove seems purely descriptive. The image of the starling as party reveller in the concluding line is charming, but presents the bird as a sort of hedonist, existing only in the moment. MacDiarmid would seldom have been so unconcerned to prove something. MacCaig observes a starling with an attentiveness which has it primarily as itself. Similarly, in his poem 'Ringed Plover at a Water's Edge', he simply presents, in an engagingly mimetic free verse, the bird. Whether one finds this valuable depends upon whether one finds Ringed Plovers valuable. The poem is unconcerned with human emotion, it has nothing to say to that part of us which expects some sort of emotional *frisson* or relevance to directly human concerns from a poem. MacCaig called such pieces 'snapshot' poems; if they are, they lack even the personal element which makes mere snapshots valuable. MacCaig's approach here seems as revolutionary as anything in MacDiarmid, albeit in a less dramatic, less showy way. He writes about such ordinary marvels as bullfinches, long-tailed tits. His vision is to regard such inhabitants of the natural world as important in themselves, not for what they may imply about humanity or the progress of humanity, but for their beautiful uselessness.

"Environment is a tremendous thing," the American poet and novelist Stephen Crane once wrote. Of Irish descent — my father was born in the Falls Road, Belfast, my mother at Maghera, County Derry, near the birthplace of Seamus Heaney — at the age of 13 I came with my family from the North of England, and settled at Cunninghamhead Estate, a caravan site, near Irvine on the west coast of Ayrshire. My father, an engineer, was moved about so frequently by his firm that we lived in a caravan which we transported to each new site. In childhood I rarely spent more than a few years in any one place. I was born, meaninglessly in all but biology, in Morecambe in 1959, but it would be truer to say I was born at Cunninghamhead. Though my genealogical origins are noticeable in the faces of my Irish cousins, Cunninghamhead is the only place I have had roots. The distinctive silhouette of Arran, in the Firth of Clyde, gray-bright on a summer evening, watermarks my mind.

Then four miles outside Irvine, Cunninghamhead Estate was, and is, a small caravan site set in ornamental grounds up a driveway quarter of a mile long, on a low hill. The Annick Water flows through the valley below it. To the west are the lavish wooded estates of Annick Lodge. It was a remark- ably sylvan environment in 1972, still bearing the airs of a more privileged time. Cunninghamhead itself had been bought, with a neighbouring farm Fairliecrevoch, for £32,850, in 1846 by one William Kerr, from Beith, whose fortune had been made on tobacco plantations in Virginia. His surviving granddaughters, both unmarried, had lived in a 'big hoose' at Cunninghamhead until the late fifties, when the house had been destroyed in a fire. Later, the ground had been bought by a local man. One of his sons tried chicken farming there unsuccessfully. But caravans worked.

When we settled near it, in 1972, Irvine had recently been designated a New Town, but few real changes had happened at that stage. My first impression of it, in November, was of gloom and darkness, but its coastal location — storms rattled in from the west — also gave it a strange glowering exhilaration. I experienced a definite culture shock. In England, despite my Irish Catholicism, I'd gone, for convenience, to Protestant schools. In Irvine I did the same. St. Michael's Academy in Kilwinning was considered too far for me to travel to. I soon discovered Irvine to be a hotbed of sectarianism. The Reformation was still ongoing there. Not notably theological, I quickly realised that 'Papes' and 'Tims' were an issue. It reminds me of a scene from a zany film I saw once, in which a sort of human flightless duck three feet tall is transported to Earth from another planet, having no knowledge of its origin. In a city one night, it spies in a television shop window a documentary about the duck-hunting season in America. On the screen, flocks of ducks fly over. The scene cuts to hundreds of duck shooters blasting them out of the air. Realisation strikes. "I'm a duck!" it says quackily, with new significance, and makes off at speed down the road, panicky and enlightened. Well, I was a duck, too. I resolved to keep it secret if possible.

Irvine's chapel, St. Mary's, was located up a side road near the school, Irvine Royal Academy. I developed a curious double life. I lived wary of discovery. I preferred winters, when I attended evening mass under cover of darkness. There was less chance then of me being spotted by my peers. In spring and summer, with their long evenings, I lived in weekly fear of my secret being revealed. I approached the chapel as furtively as a man visiting a sex shop. I couldn't invite friends up to my family's caravan at Cunninghamhead. It was too full of implicating holy relics and pictures. I grew to deeply resent the Sacred Heart that stood above the mantelpiece, gazing out imploringly with blood-dripping punctured hands. The only time I dared to ask a friend home was in the last year of school, and with someone for whom I felt it wasn't an issue. After an afternoon of birdwatching, as we waited at the bottom of the lane for the bus that would take him home, Colin MacPhee said, "Jed, are you a Catholic?" I admitted I was. "Just as well no one knew about that at the school, hey," he said gravely. The Ayrshire poet James Graham, who attended Irvine Royal as a Protestant, recently told me that the direst punishment the teacher there could threaten was the sending of a pupil to St. Michael's. The Catholic school had a dark reputation, he said. *Torture* was reputed to take place there. Obviously, problems cut both ways.

Irvine also has a number of literary connections, though they were lost on me at that stage. Its Royal Academy had a precursor which boasted Edgar Allan Poe as a temporary pupil. (The Allans were a wealthy Irvine shipping family who adopted the writer.) John Galt was born in a house on the High Street. A bank now occupies the site. Irvine also has one of the world's oldest Burns Clubs (to which, MacDiarmid, when invited, opened his peroration with: "Of course Burns wasn't a poet at all. He was a songwriter.... ") Some of the Club's founder members knew Burns personally. And the Burns Museum in the High Street houses, as well as a *Kilmarnock Edition*, the original holographs of six of that book's poems, including 'The Twa Dogs'. They all have John Wilson the printer's marks on them. Burns himself spent about a year in Irvine. He may have first discovered a copy of Robert Fergusson's poems, which influenced him greatly, in the then-Templeton's bookshop, near which over two centuries later I attended a writers' group.

In the north of England I'd gone to a new comprehensive school. Irvine Royal seemed venerable and antediluvian by comparison. Some teachers still walked round in capes and mortarboards. The boy's gym reeked of decades of accumulated sweat and agony, and classes were presided over by a pear-shaped sclerotic gym teacher with purple lightnings down the bridge of his nose. Wheezing like a steam-engine, he looked as if a walk up a flight of stairs would have induced a heart attack. In the classrooms the desks were still mainly the old-fashioned type, with inkwells. The tawse was still in use, and some teachers were reputed to be virtuosos in its deployment. One geography teacher was renowned for his habit of throwing the leather belt in the air, and catching it on its descent before executing the stroke. Occasionally I heard of pupils "refusing the belt". I was impressed, but incapable of similar rebelliousness. One art teacher was so inexpert in its use that she strapped my wrists. They were black and blue for days after.

Cunninghamhead had no one of my own age to go about with. I became a solitary. The estate was surrounded by miles of fields and woods. In England, I'd also lived on a caravan site, but one riotous with youngsters of my own age. Each spring we'd collect birds' eggs, a habit partly encouraged by the fierce competitiveness as to who would have the 'best' collection. I lacked the competitive element at 14 at Cunninghamhead, and my moral sense was developing. I became interested in the birds themselves, at first using the marvellous little *Observer's* book — even now a glance at its plates can spirit me back quarter of a century — and then saving for the *A.A. Book of British Birds,* which I bought for £4 in a bookshop in Kilmarnock. *The heron has a 'pectinated', or notched claw, which it uses to comb off eel slime after mixing it with special powdering feathers on its breast; cormorants and shags have no uropygial, or 'preen' gland, to waterproof their feathers and therefore must 'hang out' their wings to dry; the fulmar has the longest incubation period, at 51 to 53 days, of any British bird:* even 25 years later, such facts rise easily to mind.

By 15, I knew the life history and Latin name of every British bird. I would recite them, with tedious enthusiasm, at the merest suggestion of interest on the part of a listener. Terrified, with a good Irish Catholic terror, of girls, I hardly endeared myself to them with this enthusiasm in our rare contacts. They were looking for charm and banter. I was a walking ornithological computer. Lumbering and awkward in my wellington boots, I sublimated hugely in my teens.

Not always successfully. Whatever is denied grows dark and large behind the wall of its exclusion. No one is more fixated on sex than the anchorite. A half-truth perhaps, but true enough. Of one next door neighbour, ten years my senior, I later wrote:

She had what is called *it.*
Men buzzed like nervous bees when she was near.
Wordless, she electrified the atmosphere

in sea-green frock, as she would sit,
her legs demurely crossed, and sip hot coffee.
A neighbour. She was my introduction
to woman's mystery and dreamt seduction,
And I the light that couldn't escape her gravity.

My frame unfilled, a bumbling adolescent,
silk-minded, I hoped the marvel would occur
as I searched woods for nests — that I'd find her,
far from the smoky living room's covert looks.
There, her nearness charged my circuits incandescent.
And I plunged deeper into my nature books.

Perhaps, for the sake of my mental health, it is as well the 'marvel' never did occur. Would I ever have recovered?

The caravan in which we lived, though sizeable, was too small for a couple and three growing youngsters, one a 6' 2" adolescent. Lack of space drove me out of doors in all weathers. I developed, with Freudian appropriateness, a fascination for owls. I had never seen such a bird, but knew one lived in the 'witchwood' across the river. I heard it at night and found, on walks below the wood's beeches, soft wisped feathers from its breast or, occasionally, the big barred and furry-surfaced primaries. These remnants of the bird's presence fascinated me. I had no relationship with a girl; I had one with a tawny owl. I imagined I understood it. We were kindred spirits. We shared the need for secrecy. It, to catch food. I, to avoid religious martyrdom.

I read up everything about owls I could find. The Tawny Owl, Britain's commonest species, was the one heard round Cunninghamhead — the source of Shakespeare's not wholly accurate "tu-whit tu-whoo', a merry note'. (Actually two of the bird's calls conflated.) Owls swallowed their prey whole and produced, after digestion, 'pellets': gloriously glutinous accumulations of bones and fur you could find below favourite roosting sites. I would dissect these. Many contained the skulls of small rodents. According to the root pattern left when you pulled out the tiny molars in their jaws, you could tell what species the owl had been catching. Shoeboxes under my bed accumulated, containing a veritable rodent kirkyard: dissections of dozens of owl pellets. On frosty winter nights, bored with indoors, I'd take a powerful torch and go crunching across the fields: the whole universe cooling the blood in my cheeks, Orion glinting over the black barbarous hedge, redwings and fieldfares at roost rocketing out from among the thorns and assumed by glittering vastness. For fun I'd skywrite my name with the beam of the torch: a tall inverted cone of light, like an upside-down dunce's cap, ending abruptly, gliding and swooping in silence among constellations. At Annick Lodge, like the boy of Winander, and a decade before I'd heard of Wordsworth, I'd call the owls down to me with cupped hands and interlaced fingers, the big feathery blacknesses swooping sometimes to boughs just 10 feet overhead, their calls bubbling out of their throats at that distance in small liquid fountains. On my return with the night flushing my cheeks, my father would be sitting alone in darkness, watching TV, the sound turned low so as not to disturb my sleeping mother, his face ghosted by the glow of the cathode tube. He would have to rise at 6 a.m. for work. 'What did I know, what did I know,/Of love's austere and lonely offices?'

15, bird-mad, I had no interest in poetry. Then one afternoon our English teacher, Mrs MacKenzie, played us a recording of John Betjeman reading Philip Larkin's 'An Arundel Tomb'. Uncultured as a hedge, I could still recognise and respond to the pressure of experience behind Betjeman's dignified recitation. I was mocked when I owned up to it by one of my best pals, 'Chip' Cunningham (so called because his hair shone with grease a day after he washed it). I said I liked the restrained emotion in Betjeman's voice. Then, with the air of a tortoise poking its head out from its shell, he admitted he did too.

The poem my English class was studying that year, 1974, for the then 'O' Grades was Ted Hughes' 'Jaguar'. I was indifferent to the teacher's picking over of its lines, and the poem's image of the caged big cat. (I would be in my twenties before I appreciated Hughes' work.) At the back of the class one afternoon, head-down, I was idly flicking through the poetry anthology we used when I chanced upon a piece called 'Reynard's Last Run': an account, by John Masefield, of a fox being chased by hounds. As I read the strongly-rhythmical four beat couplets, I was away with that fox

> past Maesbury beech-clump grey
> that would not be green till the end of May,
> Past Arthur's Table, the white chalk boulder,
> Where pasque flowers purple the down's grey shoulder

and over those downs, and gone. I didn't know what 'downs' were. I had never heard of pasque flowers. Yet the landscape was easily transposed to that around Cunninghamhead, and I had often watched the Eglinton Hunt at Annick Lodge, its hounds bursting through a hedge and out like bees to spread over a field with their stiff upcurved tails wagging and their barks brassy. I took to reading the extract, as I later discovered it to be, for sheer pleasure in its rhythms. I can see now that it is symbolic that I should be so attracted to a poem about a fox being chased at a time when "shades of the prison house begin to close/upon the growing boy." While I recognise much in Masefield's work as sentimental, I still read parts of the fox poem with pleasure.

We sat the English 'O' level. I was too naive to play safe. I ignored 'The Jaguar', and instead wrote about 'Reynard's Last Run'. Instead of considering *Of Mice and Men,* for which we'd been given all the appropriate thoughts, I wrote about The *A. A. Book of British Birds.* In the essay section, I described the thrill of finding my first oystercatcher's nest. When we returned after the summer break, I was told I had come first in the year in the English exam. Perhaps my examiner was an ornithologist. He would certainly have been relieved at my non-conformism. However it was, I remember the distinction by virtue of its unlikelihood. My male class mates looked at me with a new lack of respect.

By early June that year, 1974, my own exams were finished. The school entered the long limbo before the summer holidays. I plunked classes. No one seemed to care, or even notice. Feeling courageous, one day I turned in at Middleton Farm, a few hundred yards down the road from Cunninghamhead. The yard was utterly silent, enlivened only by the twitterings of swallows which dived in and out of an open byre door. I knocked at the kitchen door. An old plump woman, her face contoured with wrinkles, came out with suspicion.

"Would you have any work?" I said.

"Singlin neeps." She scrutinised me. "Hae ye done that afore?"

"Yes." (I hadn't.)

"Ye ken the deefrence atween charlock an neeps?"

"Yes." (I didn't.)

"Come back the mornin. Nine o'clock. Davy'll likely stert ye."

Davy Smith, of Middleton Farm, would have been born around 1910. He lived at the farm with his two unmarried sisters, in a huge house with at least a dozen rooms. (I fantasised about living in such space.) He was a farmer of the old school: he preferred as little mechanisation as possible, and that included for singling neeps — thinning them out after sowing so each is given space to grow. The invention of the precision sower has made the job obsolete.

The following morning — a hot day — I turned up before 9 am, washed and combed, feeling vulnerable and edgy in the face of this new experience.

Davy Smith was a man of medium height. He was dressed in thick trousers kept up by braces over a brown-gold shirt with the sleeves rolled up. His powerful forearms looked disproportionately large for the rest of his body. They were scarred heavily with ringworm, which he would claw at intervals until it bled. He wore a greasy peaked cap which he would raise to scratch his wisp-haired scalp, and smile broadly, yellow stump-toothed, out of a glitter of silvery stubble. He had a habit of puffing air through his lips when troubled or considering.

It was my first experience of agriculture as it would have been practised, except for the tractor, since Burns' time.

First, he handed me two sacks, and lengths of twine.

I looked at him blankly.

"Wrap they roon yer knees Gerad," (pronounced with a hard "G") he said, "an tie them."

Singling neeps consisted of going up and down the dreels on hands and knees, or with a hoe if preferred, clearing away the excess seedlings every six inches or so. In the heat, I was soon sweating big drops that blotched the soil dark. As the ecological writer John Stewart Collis wrote, I rapidly realised the agricultural labourer's commonest question: *What is the time?* The work was sore on your spine, your knees, and your fingers, where dry earth gathered under the nails in dark crescents. Clay cutties, or pipes, occasionally come across, evidenced countless long field days down the years.

We were joined on these days by two other men: the "Miller", Davy's cousin, who lived in the defunct mill at Perceton, and Tam Lusk, a local man from the village of Springside.

The miller was a rubbery-faced man who said little except to give the time when asked for it, fishing his pocket watch out of an old waistcoat. He was teased by Davy, who obviously thought him slow.

Tam Lusk made a deep impression on me. In hot weather he would strip to the waist. He had the physique of a boxer, and I'd watch, fascinated, at the interlinking movements of the muscles as he went up and down the dreels. "Nae joab fer the human boady this," he would say. His attitude to me was one of mild protectiveness.

Davy Smith's attitude was to treat me insouciantly, and not wholly convincingly, as 'the young intellectual'. He seemed proud that he read the then *Glasgow Herald,* as if he considered this unusual for a man of his station. He had an encyclopaedic knowledge of Irvine families — something not possible now — and would quiz me about my schoolpals. Then would follow genealogies, backgrounds and occupations of their fathers and mothers.

At precisely noon every day we all stopped for lunch, and would bump back to the farmhouse on the trailer of the tractor, to enter the big cool kitchen. A cat would be up on the table, licking the butter, till growled at by Davy. His sister Mary would serve the meal, and I'd watch fascinated, with the unfeeling fascination of the young, as she stood at the sink: the flesh on her calves sagged over the top edges of her shoes, like loose trouserbottoms, and vibrated with every step. Dinner was a solemn slow affair, punctuated mainly by the clink of cutlery on china. A housefly would sit proprietorially on the edge of the butter dish, rubbing its front legs together in an action reminiscent of Fagin over a gold hoard. Davy invariably took a nap after lunch. He would lie on his back on a couch in the kitchen, the newspaper opened out over his face. It would flutter and rise each time he sighed, but he never overslept. At 1pm he would wake, grasp the paper with his right hand, sit up, and say, "Weel..."

We worked from 1pm until 5pm, with a break at 3.30pm. This was my favourite break. When you took it, you knew the day's work would soon be over. The signal for the pause was the sight of one of Davy's sisters, approaching through the heat shimmer across the field, carrying a basket with sandwiches and tea in a tin flask. We'd all walk slowly up to the shade of the hedge. The combination of weariness and the open air made these afternoon breaks the most refreshing I have known. The tea seemed better than any I'd ever tasted. There was a glow about us as we sat in silence. Sometimes there'd be banter.

"Ye'll be a man fer the weemun, then," Davy said to me once. He grinned, yellowly.

"Eh?" I said, affecting ignorance.

"The weemun. The lassies."

"Not really."

"Gie im time," said Tam Lusk. "He's jist a buoy yet, Christ."

"The miller's a man fer the weemun," said Davy. "They aw think he's braw, dain't they miller?"

"Oh aye," the miller said, not realising he was being mocked. "Some o them, onywey."

"Best tae stey awa fae them," said Tam Lusk with saturnine conviction. (I later learned he had numerous children.) "They're naethin but boather."

That summer I also helped with hay work. Davy came up to summon me, causing a minor stir by clumping up the path in his hob-nailed boots and asking my mother, "Gerad in, missus?" Tam Lusk was there again, and youths from Springside. We were joined by a red-headed woman of about 30 from a neighbouring farm. She had a loud manner, and was attractive in a robust way. Her full breasts vibrated eyecatchingly below her sweater as she walked round. Her presence introduced a new atmosphere among the men, myself, at 15, included. They developed a canine wariness and edginess, glossed over with banter.

"Whit wid ye dae tae that, hey?" one of them said to me, when her back was turned. Not forthcoming in frank sexual talk with other men at that age, I made one or two affirming noises. This seemed to convince him of my acceptibility.

Later, in the barn, the men talked about her reputation for sexual licence. One said, "Aye, Davy says he fun the pair o them in the barn, jeans roon their ankles, gaun at it like rabbits." Then, addressing me, he added, "keep yer eye on er, son. She'll hae the breeks aff ye in saiconts."

Everyone laughed. In an attempt to divert attention from this impugning of my inexperience I recounted an incident in the byre one Saturday morning. I had been mucking it out when Meg, Davy Smith's second sister, burst in, grabbed the shovel from me, and for half a minute furiously scraped and emptied the wet sloppy dung into the wheelbarrow. "That's hoo ye dae it!" she hissed, and exited like a destroyer.

"Pey nae attention, son," Tam Lusk said. "She's needin a man." The ultimate answer to all the woes of womankind.

Two chance encounters led to the taking of the photographs in this book, and the writing of its poems — if chance isn't a misnomer. We gravitate like plants to light toward self-realisation. As Robert Frost wrote, in 'Snow': "Our very life depends on everything's/ Recurring till we answer from within./ The thousandth time may prove the charm."

One afternoon, from Irvine harbourside, I saw people walking the mudflats across the river. They could only have been, I surmised, birdwatching. Kindred spirits! I took my bicycle and pedalled energetically the several mile detour round, to meet them.

They turned out to be two remarkable brothers, living in Irvine with their parents. They were, respectively, ten and seven years older than me, with interests in natural history and photography, and they welcomed me in the months after like a third brother. We made an impassioned triumvirate, loud and boisterous as young men are, but rarely crude. We seldom, as far as I recall, discussed sex or women. We exclaimed over bird photographs in copies of *The Encyclopaedia of Birds* as loudly as other young males would have over photographs in *Penthouse*. We discussed lenses and their quality with rampant lust. They talked of going on 'expeditions' to this island or that, to Madagascar, to the Galapagos. I had never heard such adventurous talk before. They were Romantics, Wordsworthians without having read Wordsworth. Hitherto, my response to nature had been fascinated but factual. Influenced by them, I was soon a full-blown Romantic myself. We competed mainly in the enthusiasm with which we expressed our delight in nature. By a process of osmosis, I took up nature photography in my late teens. A six month spell in the first winter after I left school in a 'job creation' factory, spent mainly pop-riveting metal boxes, or 'gardening' — a euphemism for digging over a patch of ground repeatedly — earned me £22 a week, from which I saved for my first serious camera, an Olympus OM1. We planned and carried out various 'projects', among them the photography of short-eared owls at the nest in Ayrshire, and a three week spell spent on the uninhabited island of Eilean Hoan, off the coast of Sutherland, where we photographed gulls and other birds.

By the time I was a labourer working at Inverkip power station, where I lugged bales of rocksil insulation to scaffolding sites, I had decided to try and become a freelance. I learnt that it was often easier to sell photographs if you supplied them with articles. I began writing nature journalism. Leafing through the *Writers and Artists' Yearbook* I discovered that the highest paying market in Britain — I was sadly mercenary in those days — was *Reader's Digest*. It paid, at that time, £1,000 an article. I pestered one of their editors for months with queries and articles deemed unsuitable but promising, articles with titles like "Meet the Happy Hedgehog". Eventually, the long-suffering editor suggested I could write them a piece about bats. For the next three weeks I lived, slept, and dreamt bats. They accepted the piece, after some quibbles, and I wrote them another, this time on kestrels, which they also accepted. Shortly after, they flew me to London to meet them. An innocent abroad, I survived, though my caravan was translated instantly to a 'mobile home' by the Assistant Editor to make it more acceptable to the Editor-in-Chief. Soon I was able to become a full-time freelance, frequently castigated by them for including too many Scottish references.

By then the former triumvirate had broken up. The brothers had left the area. One had got married. My interest in photography had peaked. My interest in writing was growing.

A few years before, I had met Sam Gilliland, a writer who lived in the last house on the edge of Springside, a local mining village with an unemployment rate of around 50%. Springside is not noted for its literary culture. I would walk through it reading a book. "Haw mister, is that the Bible?" the weans would ask.

Sam Gilliland impressed me with his devotion to writing. I was intrigued by the little that satisfied him. A good line, a good poem, and he was happy. He would talk of having typed so much of a novel he had to bandage up his wrists. There was a glamour associated with the potentially huge earnings even an unknown writer could, conceivably, win. Hope was in the air. An autodidact like myself, Sam was among the sharpest men, in fundamental things, I had met. An engineer by training, he had a wide knowledge of many practical matters, this crossed with a strong and unusually selfless interest in poetry and an emotional generosity rare among men, with other men. I would pass his house late on snell nights in the autumn and see him at work in the lit uncurtained cell of his front room, hammering out prose on a manual typewriter of piano-like dimensions: a small figure with, above the roof, out in the Universe, the Pleiades sparkling softly, like a considering brain.

Sam's persistence and self-sufficiency attracted me. Impressed, and following the breaking open of my sensibility by my falling in love for the first time, I began trying to write poetry. My first attempts would not have inspired confidence, had I known any better. But bliss was it to be ignorant, seeking the one rapture of an inspiration. "I feel again that joy,/" I wrote, "Whose fiery flames can shoot/ An arrow of passion through my brain."

Visual images, whether paintings or photographs, have often fed poetry. The wistful poem based on a photograph of a dead relative is now a cliché, almost irrespective of quality. There is something about the documentary element of a photograph which touches and draws us. *This existed,* it says. *This was real.* The shutter opens and closes, and within the dark box, through the magic of light which has travelled from a star 93 million miles off in space, or from a flash tube ten feet distant, an image is captured. 'But O, Photography, as no art is, which will not censor..." wrote Philip Larkin, in 'Lines on a Young Lady's Photograph Album'. It is not altogether true. The camera may not lie, but the lens can be directed, the light manipulated.

In one sense at least, a photograph is like a poem: it can focus on a particular aspect of its subject. Its frame excludes and emphasises. It is a perfect means for documenting the natural world. While it doesn't entirely negate the concept of photographer as artist, its technical aspects are a given. One doesn't need an innate gift in those to the degree that, say, a portrait artist does. The equipment, to an extent, does it for you, and the result has the advantage of representing the natural world 'as it really is'.

Some of the pictures here were taken in Argyll and Sutherland, but most were taken in Ayrshire, and within a 30 mile radius of Cunninghamhead. I knew the ground. I knew what to find, where and when. Green Tiger Beetles stalked the hot sand in April at Shewalton Sand Pits near Irvine. In May there were Fragrant Orchids in the hills above Dundonald. The rock pools at Portencross were natural aquaria of pellucid clarity where I could come across Dahlia anemones, blennies, or prawns picking their way delicately over the coralline on the pools' sides. There was a small pond on old mine workings at Sevenacres near Kilwinning where dragonfly and damselfly nymphs could be found crawling up reed stems to hatch into adults.

It is difficult to be romantic about nature now. The tremendous success of the American cartoonist Gary Larson, with his neo-Darwinist comic take on the ruthlessness of the natural world, is symptomatic of this modern attitude. Nature's buoyant ooriness is emphasised down among the stems and the antennae with a macro lens. The 'higher' animals can be said to share some characteristics in common with humans, but the more 'primitive' the creature the more emphasised its otherness. Anyone who has experienced silent hordes of clegs on a remote road, their attentiveness and persistence, and the impression they give of an intelligence not so much malign but indifferent, and therefore more sinister, will need no convincing of that. Edwin Muir, in his book *Scottish Journey,* gives a remarkable account of such an episode. Around his faulty, open-topped car in a remote glen in Sutherland, while his hands were occupied, the clegs drifted in a cloud, before alighting upon the poet and his vehicle. "When I felt the horrible creatures crawling over my lips," he wrote, "I became flustered." As well he might.

There is also something aweing about the purposefulness of all those chitin jaws, those wings, those quivering antennae. Last summer, a species of solitary wasp used a cleft in the stonework of Brownsbank beside the door to nest in. What did it know of MacDiarmid? What did it know of me as I sat scribbling this? The neo-Darwinists believe that, in evolutionary terms, to nature a human being is of no greater or lesser value than, say, an emperor moth, a gnat, or a gem anemone. This may disturb those with a hierarchical view of the natural order. I have sometimes found it consoling. We are not as important as we think we are. The world, the 'creation', could get on fine without us. The Solitary Wasp may inherit the earth. All that matters to the life force is the love that moves the earth and the other planets — a fierce and horrific love sometimes, but perhaps love nonetheless. Not even the atoms of our bodies belong to us. We only have them on loan. They are recycled, they go round, they come around, in their endless permutations. As Primo Levi traced, thrillingly in *The Periodic Table,* atoms are epic travellers. Some atoms of me as I write this could have been, or could be again, found in the antennae of a beetle, or the compound eye of a dragonfly, or the palps of a male spider, or high in an oak, rustling in one of its many leaves over human heads. According to Vincent Cronin in his book *Man Looks At the Cosmos,* every human being at birth contains three grams of gold. This was forged, suggests modern astronomy, in the tremendous heat of the great explosion of a distant star, from which explosion was formed the material of which our solar system was made. As the Dumfries poet Kirkpatrick Dobie once wrote: "I am the stuff of stars/ For what else can I be?"

MacDiarmid in one of his poems praised photography for its fidelity to fact. The challenge when writing poems to accompany pictures is to make imaginative reality out of hard fact, as well as, with specialist subjects, to elucidate the content of the photograph. Also, though it is intended that picture and poem be considered together, and they form, viewed thus, a greater whole than separately, one is attempting to make the poems stand alone as works in their own right.

We will doubtless never know what insects' and other creatures' perception of the world is. The most one can do is elucidate the findings of science as it reveals their lives to us. The device of assuming the persona of a creature, as I have adopted here at times, has a lineage which goes back as far as Anglo-

Saxon, and its riddles. In Anglo-Saxon times, people living cheek by jowl with nature could not easily forget that the world was full of other living things, presumed to be individual personalities. Bookworms, swans, onions, moon and sun and ice, are all given voice in the Anglo-Saxon world. It's a tradition poets have often fed on: Ted Hughes' justly famous 'Hawk Roosting', as well as writing by Scottish poets such as Edwin Morgan and Brian McCabe, continue the tradition.

Keats felt that the beauty of a rainbow was somehow tarnished by knowledge of its properties. Yet the natural world is surely made more, not less, marvellous by awareness of its workings. In the poems that accompany these pictures, I have tried to give an inkling of that. May the marriage of verse and image enlarge the reader's appreciation and, perhaps, insight into, the chomping, scurrying, quivering, procreating and dying kingdom, however many miles it be beyond the door.

Gerry Cambridge
Brownsbank Cottage
May 1999

Head of Common Frog

He's tasty and he knows it,
you would think, by how he looks —
distinctly nervous,

                  each eye

placed as high

                  as a sentry

on the small hill of his head —
to scan on every side
for foxes, badgers, owls, the snide
stateliness
of the assassin
Heron.

The kiss of the sweetest princess
means less
than spiders and flies to him.

Heroic
in unimpressiveness,
steadfast,
stoic,
he will try
nonetheless
to escape till the end,

the small green Sisyphus
whose stone
is life.

Head of COMMON FROG: using specially mounted eyes, the Common Frog, *Rana temporaria*, needs to be more vigilant than the toad; lacking poison glands in the skin, it is much more palatable than its wartier cousin. The bulging eyes are also of use when the frog catches prey: when it swallows, by reflex action the eyes descend into the roof of the mouth, and help force the food to the back of the frog's throat.

Fritillary Wing

Upbuckler of bens,
fashioner of stars,
of the sun's unimaginable
violence exploding the dark's
reign, of the shark's
fang and the eagle's hooks,
of the muscular
pump of the human heart,
the pipes of the aorta,
the tough tonnage of the elephant,
and the bloodstream roar of the blue whale —

micro-jeweller, too,
of a billion wings of butterflies,
each perfect in their pattern,
their lines of glittering dust set down
scale by inscribed scale.

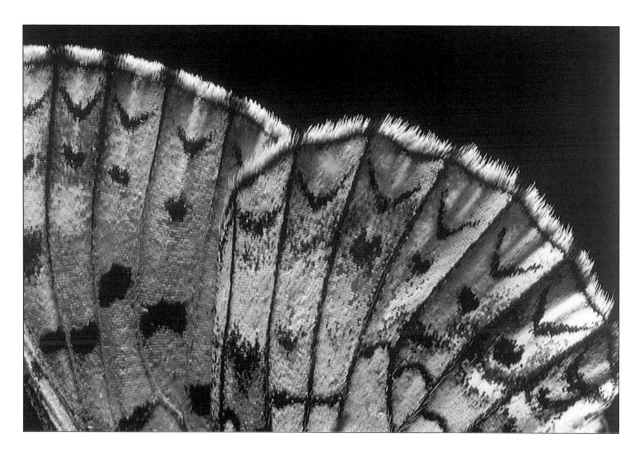

FRITILLARY WING: fine dust that comes off as powder on one's fingers after handling a butterfly is in fact the microscopic scales on its wings. Arranged like roof-slates, they give each species its unique pattern. Each scale is a tiny flattened bag with a short stalk which fits into a socket on the wing membrane. Only butterflies and moths, among insects, possess scales. The *Lepidoptera*, their zoological grouping, is derived from the Greek *lepis (scale)* and *pteron (wing)*. This photograph was taken using a mounted specimen. Size of original: *3 centimetres*.

Common Lizard

One hundred and sixty million years of dinosaurs
has left in Scotland
you,
diminutive,
like living proof that they did live,
Tyrannosaurus, Triceratops,
in the unimaginable world
before human laws and tax and schools and shops —
you, no dinosaur in size
except to the spiders and the flies
you prey on in the summer, your scaled skin
a mosaic as of polished pebbles
inset by a master craftsman.
A perfect miniature, then, breathtaking —
your movement so fast it outwits the eyes
in this world of giant women and men
whose force you must bow to among
the August grasses and the stony slopes of the ben.
The scales are all reversed.
It is human feet that approaching shake earth now.

The COMMON LIZARD,
Lacerta vivipara, is found throughout most of
Scotland, often to be seen sunning itself on
banks and stones — basking helps it to
synthesise vitamin D, which its body cannot
manufacture unaided. The slow-worm is
closely related, but doesn't resemble a
miniature dinosaur in that it lacks legs, or has
only vestigial ones. Lizards feed on spiders
and flies. Size: *up to 10 cm*

Sphagnum Moss

Varicoloured moss,
cushion for snipe and sundew,
you'll be peat in a millennium.
A sponge for Scotland's rains,
there is nothing aggressive in you.
You don't even resist my feet.
Mary, Queen of Scots,
supposedly employed —
to wipe her royal bum
and stanch her royal blood
seeping from the kingdom —
your gentle pink and green
in the days before modernity.
What a striking combination:
you in your lowliest station,
and Scotland's queen.

The dead leaves and stems of
SPHAGNUM form peat,
eventually. Extremely absorbent,
the moss can hold up to 20 times
its weight in water. The water
closet at Traquair House,
Scotland's oldest inhabited house,
where Mary Queen of Scots
stayed occasionally, has a plaque
concerning the use of sphagnum
for the purposes noted in the
poem. Dried sphagnum has also
been used for surgical dressings,
nappies, lamp-wicks, bedding,
and stable litter.

Bluebells

I know the glory of God by it
Hopkins wrote of the bluebell
from the edge of his private hell.
The blue buzzed-haze and the wafts
of intoxicant perfume
must have seemed glory indeed
from the tight mahogany room
of celibate theology.
                    The flower itself
has no soul or pretence of one,
it will merely live and die
in its swaying thousands
of stamens and anthers and milken stems,
a perch for the satisfied fly.

A paradigm of art —
this grace of blue,
conjured out of the moil
of roots and rotting leaves and mite-stirred soil.

BLUEBELLS. Gerard Manley Hopkins, one of Britain's finest nature poets, wrote this in his journal about the Bluebell, *Endymion non-scriptus,* in the happy period before he produced his *Terrible Sonnets* and, later, stopped writing poetry altogether.

Male Emperor Moth, Newly-Emerged

The Emperor Moth
who flies at speed
over moors
by day,
a speck across the eye,
hasn't the time to feed
(he has no mouth),
but only to follow the planet's
way — to find a female,
breed,
and die.

Scotland is not his country
though he's made of it down to his scales.
He'll fly no flag but that of his unfurled wings.
Soon he'll be gone, on his quest —

a world of Emperor Moths the best of Grails.

MALE EMPEROR MOTH: thirty-five minutes before this picture was taken, this moth had emerged from its chrysalis: the wings are not yet fully extended. Its feathery antennae are used to 'scent' a female *(see Luna Moth, following page)*. The Emperor Moth is day-flying and common in Scotland. Bring an unmated female to a moor in a jam jar, puncture holes in the lid, and wait, and in a few minutes, seemingly from nowhere, numerous males will arrive to mate with her.

Luna Moth Antennae

Sex is what I mean
says the Luna Moth, eternal optimist, *with my*
extravagant ferns of antennae,
my DNA quills,
the quivering mothy technology
flash as the stag's antlers —
radar to sense ripe females in the night,
the atoms of pheronome
floating their signal, the secret
just for me. They are out there, they are out there,
fluttering
in the wilderness of air, and I go —
an arrow under the constellations. No star is peak*
of my desire, but the fat furred females
packed with eggs I brave the tremendous miles to seek.

*'The desire of the moth for the star' –Shelley

This picture is included in the interests of internationalism, and represents the only species not found in Scotland in this book. The male LUNA MOTH, of America, like its Scottish relative the Emperor, uses enormous antennae to scent a female, sometimes to a distance of up to 11 kilometres.

Foxgloves

Come now, bees, you want to, don't you?
Why else am I here in my purplish-red,
stately and tall at the dark wood's edge?
With the leopard spots on my petals' lips
I will draw you in, with the silk
of my every gloving bell
enclose you well
in your deep desire for the sticky drops
in my shaking steeple.
Yes, thrum and vibrate in my bells
my buzzing loves, I'll dust your hair
with the glorious gold that's a half of life
in return for your clumsy lust! Yes,
visit my softness again and again,
do not be put off by wind and rain —
let me slenderly spring in my satin dress
for your kin for a thousand summers,
my bells all trembling in the air's caress.

Known as 'Dead Old Women's Fingers' or 'Witch's Fingers' in Gaelic, the FOXGLOVE, *Digitalis purpurea,* is poisonous, though cultivated commercially for the heart-stimulating drug Digitalis, made from its dried leaves.

Puffball Dispersing Spores

Raindrops
are the puffball's lovers.
In the wet wood, day or night,
they drip their good
weight of water;
and the spores explode
from the opened tops
and waft away, each so light
that in motionless air
one can take half an hour to fall through inches.
They waft away
joining the drifting hosts,
the silent billions
unseen in the air about us —
till suddenly
thickened from water,
a puffball's

there.

PUFFBALLS are common British fungi, edible
when fresh, when they resemble marshmallow
in texture. Later they dry to a dusty mass of
spores, a process which opens a 'vent' in the
top of the fungi for the spores to escape.
In this photograph, raindrops, falling on the
puffball, cause the spores to puff out into the
air. The largest species in Scotland, the giant
puffball, *Lycoperdon giganteum*, can grow to
half a metre across.

Fly Agaric

The Vikings
were said to chew you for battle frenzy.
The Lapps
believed that you sprang
from the blood-flecked foam
of Odin's steeds
as they thundered across the sky.
As if you were wholly imaginary
in the weans' books
there'd be elves always about you,
bogills and glaistigs and kelpies haunted
the woods and the waters too,
though I'm more knowledgeable now,
know you're just spores in the birchwood,
teeming miraculous dust
feeding upon the dead.

A fungal kirkyard,
a feast for the slow
silent
processions of slugs ...

Yet strange to find
your gothic dozens — as if
I'd ventured back into some fairy tale —
in their actual white and red.

FLY AGARIC causes intoxication
and sickness if eaten, though it's
not fatal to man. It is usually
found in birchwoods. Fungi such
as this lack chlorophyll to make
their own food, and so live on
organic matter in the soil. They
reproduce by spores — tiny dust-
like seeds which drift down from
between the 'gills' on the plant's
underside. Each of these fungi in
the picture will produce at least
several million such spores,
though only a tiny number ever
form new specimens.

Seeds of *Betula pendula* (Birch)

We're the seeds of the birks —
with our warm gold hearts
our fecundity
matches the strictures of chapels and kirks.
Each of us here a sealed envelope
containing the intricate letter
of earthly hope —
'hope' 's too strong, rather of instinct —
our parent writes in millions and millions and millions.
The wind is our postman,
the hands that open us water and heat and light,
the recipient
may be sheugh or tarmac or the good ground
where we'll thresh and glitter in the world's air
half a century hence, fresh emerald
on the blue
and the towery white.
Open us up and you'd not see packed
the skinkling leaves and the silver bark —
yet they are there, infolded and hidden
like your own future,
the starry genes in the cell of the dark.

SILVER BIRCH seeds usually hang in catkins and are dispersed by the wind. Each seed here would be around *4-5mm* across. The little 'wings' on each side of the seed increase the surface area by which the wind may propel it.

Large Elephant Hawkmoth at Dusk

Night is my kingdom,
night and flight.
I wait, for now,
antennae laid back,
wings still,
in my pink and lime plush,
my furriness, that will
go birring around
your ears in oorie dark
raising with sound the hairs on your nape.

You cannot know me:
I am not to be known,
though you have found me
by chance.
I shall never be back here again.
In minutes I shall have flown.

The LARGE ELEPHANT HAWKMOTH,
Deilephila elpenor, takes its name from the
caterpillar's habit of rearing up and extending
the front of its body like an elephant's trunk if
threatened. Disturbed by day, the moth
squirts a white liquid over the fingers. The
caterpillars feed only on Rosebay Willowherb,
a common wild flower. Size: *4-5cm.*

Waiting for Sun

So delicate — in the still
dreich noon on the heathery slope
of this Argyll hill —

it is like coloured air
too frail to bend the stem
it has alighted on. There

it waits for a beam —
the Small Pearl-bordered Fritillary —
incendiary brilliance or the merest gleam

as it hides in the huge
library of the land, in its
unstirring subterfuge.

A pristine miniature volume
of instructions for butterfly making,
poised on the heather's bloom.

One break in the cloud, and look —
the sun in his coat of light will enter
and softly open these wings like a book.

The SMALL PEARL BORDERED
FRITILLARY butterfly rests on
flowers in dull summer weather,
when it's so tame you can lift it
on a fingertip. The slightest blink
of sun, however, and it flies off,
to mate and feed. Nine species of
fritillary are found in Britain. This
one was found on a hill slope
beside a forestry track in Argyll.
Size: *3cm.*

Head of the Common Cleg

I am the cleg,
the bloodsucking female —
professor or pauper
you're nothing to me but a factory of blood on legs.

I think just of my eggs,
I need blood-protein.
Hot blood, the best, no dregs,
I come with my armoured mouth for,
my stabbing dirk,
and I am sly.

I fly
silent, alight,
silent, duskily-winged.

I am the mother, I am nature,
all that I care for's my progeny.

I see you as movement
with my rainbowed eyes,
the one vertical on the sunstruck moor.
On the road from Cape Wrath to the Kyle,
the oorie calm
of my kind,
our silent persistence,
our whirling clouds
un-nerved you,
who's nothing to us.

And nothing can stop us trying for blood,
to death we follow that path
to our living armies, indifferent
to all but that, below the indifferent blue.

This big close up offers an eerie glimpse into the world of the CLEG. Only female horseflies suck blood. The males are pollen feeders. Much less common now than formerly, owing to modern agricultural methods, clegs have compound eyes especially good for detecting movement. The eyes' bands of iridescence fade rapidly after death. Size of cleg: *c. 12mm.*

Short Eared Owl Settling on Eggs, Sitka Spruce Plantation

In miles of sapling spruce
she settles,
small in those miles as a comma in a book,
the bird of hooks and big plush softness,
her eyes of fire
across two decades
outstaring the viewer's look.

Both she and her chicks long dead,
in a thirtieth of a second then
in Clauchriehill plantation
the shutter clicked and locked her
like a trophy of light in the magic box,
so here in your sight she lives again
in her fierce motherhood
before politics, geography, nation.

The SHORT-EARED OWL, *Asio flammeus,* takes its name
from little feather tufts above the eyes, which are only
visible when the bird is relaxed. The real ears are huge, and
found under skin flaps on each side of the bird's facial disc.
It flies and hunts by day, often nesting in spruce plantations
where its favourite prey, the short-tailed vole, is abundant.
Its characteristic slow quartering flight is unmistakeable. It
will attack humans who venture near the nest once the
chicks have hatched.

Head of Great Black-Backit Gull

The great black-backit gull
has no concept of mercy in mind at all,
except in regard to its chicks perhaps;
I've seen it feeding the small
fluff-bundles, stump-winged, tenderly
from the tip of the pickaxe beak.

'Wicked big characters them,' Michael would say —
if one can attribute morals to a bird that may
not know, for instance, that it exists,
so remarked my friend the philosopher.
The eider ducklings that were part of its prey
were incapable of such speculation.
I would watch a pair of these gulls
round the island coast
quarter above an eider duck with her brood,
sending them this way and that
in sheer panic till they singled one out from the rest.
And down one would swoop
on the duckling and pluck it
head-first out of the waves,
alight on a nearby rock
and swallow the bird in a gulp.
For a moment you'd see,
sticking out from each side at the base of the beak,
each little webbed foot, hapless, weak.

At some *.75 metres* in length the GREAT
BLACK-BACKIT GULL is Scotland's biggest
species of gull. The red spot on the lower
beak is a stimulant to the chicks; when they
peck it, the adult regurgitates food for them.
The adult gulls eat almost anything, but eider
ducklings are among their favourite prey.

Eider Duck

Brown, maternal brown,
All curves but for her beak,
While the dandified male randans
The female Eider
Cradles her big green eggs
On eiderdown.

For a month her rounded breast
Heats them into life;
Even to feed she'll seldom
Leave unless coerced:
This one was so reluctant to
I could stroke her on the nest.

She'd turn and peck
My fingers perfunctorily
As if it were out of character —
Aggression.
But, being forced, she showed it,
Jerking her brown neck.

Suddenly, one day,
She was a modest liner
Flanked by dependent tugboats
Braving the massive beaks
(With their own chicks to feed)
In the glinting bay.

The FEMALE EIDER incubates for 30 days, plucking eider down from her breast to line the nest. *(The down has been commercially harvested in Iceland.)* The female also raises the young alone. Few survive *(see page 55)*. This picture was taken on Eilean Hoan, Sutherland. The female may incubate for days at a time. When she leaves the nest to feed, she covers the eggs with her down.

Newly-Hatched Herring Gull Chicks

He came out after his blow-dried
brothers (or sisters) —
he's shattered, a sodden mite.
All he can do is slump in a heap
with his down still drookit from the ooze of the egg,
but not to sleep.
Life starts here,
with its endlessness
(for him).
Give him an hour or two.
He'll be dried by the sea-breeze, tittivated up
like his siblings
and (which is why they crouch)
perilously
new.

GULL CHICKS: This picture was taken on Eilean Hoan, Sutherland. Gulls nest in large colonies, and the chicks are *nidifugous:* able to leave the nest not long after hatching. The little white dot on the tip of the beaks of the two dried chicks here is the 'egg-tooth', which each used to chip its way from the egg.

Blue Damselfly

Damsel in delicacy yes you are
but a horror with whiskered jaws
to what you feed on — midges, gnats;
as distance permits the beauty of a star,
your frailty disguises the natural law.
In dozens against the black
depths of a canal, you're each some psychedelic
spaceship in your microworld, improbable
tiny craft of turquoise light,
whirring without noise.
How easily you're grounded! All night
on leaf and blade your thousands
of stripes of airy blue,
the intricate battalions,
wait for the sun, master technologist,
to rise white from the mist
and slacken your chains of dew.

Damselflies are smaller versions of dragonflies, though weaker fliers. This species, the COMMON BLUE DAMSELFLY, *Coenagrion puella,* is found around ponds and canals throughout Scotland in summer.

Four Spot Libellula

The biggest dragonfly ever
had a wingspan of over two feet,
but there's no chance now you will meet
its rustle and glint around
your head in glen or glade. It has been dead
for millions of years, coal such as that
I toss on the fire has taken the print
of its wings. But here's
its modern relative,
poised on a stem and resting
from its stratagem — to quarter round
a territory snatching the flies and bees
with its basket of six spined legs,
its eyes with their thousands of facets
that emphasise many-fold the slightest movement,
its wings like the brittlest cellophane
stretched over frost-stiffened nets,
and whatever it has for brain
delicately primed.
                    Once at the edge of a wood
one alighted on the yellow wool
of the sweater on my chest; mesmerised I stood
peering down as it swivelled its head
and was gone again in a glim of wings
into its timeless future.
And I walked on — to it, at most,
put to brief use as a resting post.

Dragonflies existed some 300 million years ago. This FOUR SPOT LIBELLULA, *Libellulla semiquadrimaculata,* is common in Scotland. It has a wing span of some *7-8cm,* and will live for about a month. The huge eyes are particularly good at detecting movement. Multi-faceted, those of a big dragonfly may contain up to 30,000 such ommatidia.

'Mask' of Aeshna Juncea

This is the view from below
of the head
of the cast skin of a dragonfly nymph,
the Common Aeshna's, a husk
two inches long you can find
on summer mornings at the pond's fringes,
clinging to reeds and near-translucent then,
perfect
but for the hole in the back
where the dragonfly emerged —
a frail ghost, a papery monument
to four years crawling in mud and gloom and weed.
Millions of them in ponds each winter! —
creeping like sluggish spiders,
a leg, and a leg, and a leg,
searching for prey. Those
translucent bubbles held the eyes,
and you can see, efficiently folded
under the head
the hinged lower jaw it shot out
hydraulically pressured
(as a hosepipe straightens with the force of water)
and the two curved spikes at the end
to hook its prey, tadpole, frog, whatever
moved, down in the world of lower day
to suck out the bodily juices.
So many anonymous deaths
so that primping in the light
the dragonfly in its small splendour
could emerge and rustle away!

This is the nymph of *Aeshna juncea,* the COMMON AESHNA, one of Scotland's biggest dragonflies, measuring around *10cm* across the wings. The nymph, which grows to around *50mm*, is a predator in ponds. The 'mask', clearly visible here, is a development of the lower jaw.

Birth of Sympetrum Dragonfly

When the dragonfly's ready to hatch,
its nymph crawls out of its pond
into what must seem the beyond
to it, locks its legs round the reed-stems,
and is still as if it's dead.
The sun has risen. Two hours since dawn.
This morning in June as the light
enters the kitchens and people yawn
round the breakfast tables
here, near the base of the head,
the skin of the nymph will split
and the dragonfly-to-be
shoves back through it,
and hangs down, legs in the air,
by its still-unexpanded abdomen. Till
like a gymnast it lurches up and grips
the cast skin, pulls
its body clear, like a man easing up
through a syver ——
the wet shrivelled wings
to be pumped with air
and the big eyes still
to swell to their final size.
So it rests, fills out,
its wrinkles vanish
as people drive off to work
or enter the gates to school
in the rays of the fresh new day.
An hour or two and the dragonfly
is ready for the air. Can you imagine it ——
to split your skin down your spine and step clear,
wings on your back like an angel's to be shaken out
and take you away over rooftops, fields, and hills?
Our world is the dragonfly's heaven.

This DRAGONFLY, *Sympetrum striolatum,* would have spent perhaps two years underwater as a nymph. In this photograph, the cast skin is clearly visible; the new dragonfly is clinging to it. The metamorphosis can be seen on summer mornings at the edge of favoured ponds. The new dragonfly here is around *4cm* in length.

Head of Great Diving Beetle,
Dytiscus marginalis

He's coming for you, tadpole,
he's coming for you, newt,
and for you, stickleback, and you —
if you've flesh enough for him —
so be on the watch, astute.
You are his life, the vital goal
he takes as unquestioned due.
For that face, they invented 'grim'.
The opposite of cute,
he comes out of nowhere, fast,
breenges in like a drunken giant —
it's no use being defiant —
to make you the past
with his stabbing jaws
and his horny hug,
his armour shining like a stomping boot.
He knows of no enemy, needs no friend.
He's coming for you, tadpole,
he's coming for you, newt.
Flesh is his only goal.
He'll find us out, in the end.

The adult DYTISCUS, like its larva, feeds by injecting digestive juices into its prey and sucking out the contents. It grows to around *4cm* in length, lives in ponds, and spreads from pond to pond by flying. It will eat anything it can catch and overcome. It dives by means of its paddle-like legs, and breathes by using air stored below its 'elytra', or wing cases.

Common Toads in Amplexus

Poor toads. It cannot be much of a life.
To have your guts squeezed out
through your mouth on roads
or skulk in the damp
to flick out your sticky
tongue at a passing beetle.
Even their mating's strife.
Each so ugly, it is a form of beauty,
in their hundreds they come in spring
over fields and roads to the favourite ponds,
a carnival of hops,
diminutive males
outnumbering
females sometimes by ten to one.
She is enormous with eggs.
He has grown pads on his 'thumbs', for holding on.
No boudoir delicacy here
but a riot, attempted rape — she
may be buried below
a ball of croaking males
but if she's lucky, and he,
somehow it ends like this —
his clinging to her for life,
sometimes so tightly
she is left with wounds from his desperate grip.
But neither of them is important then —
only the eggs in their thousands
wound like jellied strings
round sunken stems,
and ticking like minute clocks
towards hatching's
kingdom.

The COMMON TOAD, *Bufo bufo*, can live for up to 10 years. Mainly nocturnal, it lives in damp places by day. It eats beetles, ants, snails, worms, caterpillars, catching them with its sticky darting tongue. A toad may travel up to a mile to reach its mating pond. The female may lay up to 7,000 eggs there, in long glutinous strings wound round underwater weeds.

Great Water Boatman

Patiently
I'm waiting for feasts to fall
on my table of water,
the surface of the pond I hang from
with the air at my abdomen's tip
buoying me.

Let them blunder,
alight for slaughter: they'll find
water's not solid
and jerk, thrash, send
out ripples I'll sense
with the spikes of my feet
and glide towards with my strong legs' paddles,

efficient oarsman,
towards their end
at my piercing beak.

I'll suck the bodies dry
of spider, gnat, or fly.
I live, and they must die.

Notonecta glauca, the GREAT WATER
BOATMAN, has a long beak, visible here,
folded back, for stabbing its prey. It remains
attached to the underside of the water surface
by means of air trapped below its wing cases
— for it can also fly, from pond to pond.
The water surface is visible here as the thin
line near the top of the picture. In life, the
insect measures *c. 2cm* across its paddle-like
front legs.

Fallen Maple Leaves

Like jigsaw pieces to an unfound puzzle,
drawn up from where we lie now we were each
a bud that swayed on the blue and white,
then made all summer a submarine shade
with our rustling high society. Now we
are colours of blood and butter and bronze,
wind-shaken down from our lofty tree,
and not to be shamed by our last flamboyance
before we re-enter mud's democracy.

FALLEN MAPLE LEAVES in October at Blair
Estate, Ayrshire.

Veins and Carotene Pigment
in a Maple Leaf

These are my channels,
my tiny canals,
my lightning for water, skeleton of vessels
for the push of the sea
that unfurled the buds
on my parent tree and spread me
silken and flimsy at first
to sun and to rain and wind.
Ah my incredible network —
intricate as the eyes' capillaries —
what miles of it in a forest!
Were it a writing
what books it would fill,
what arboreal libraries
repeating the same live fact.
Now I am old, my chlorophyll gone,
I blaze out in red like the hair of a feisty woman,
in the late splendour of the carotene.
I shall soon be dead
and the winter tree will forget me,
already dreaming of spring
and the aerial miles of green.

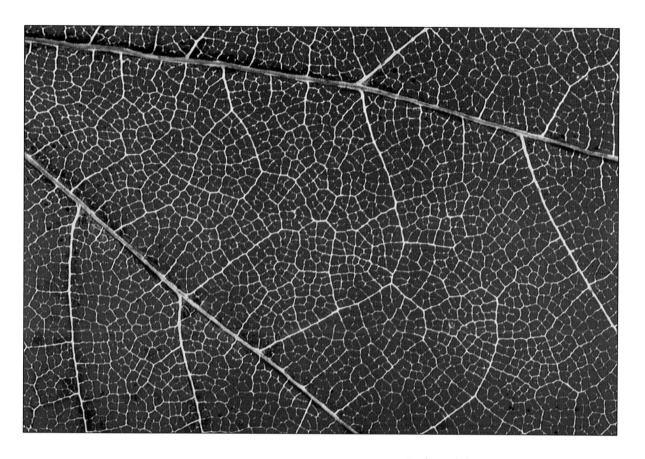

Leaf veins help to transport water from the roots of the tree to the leaves, as well as food made in the leaves, during photosynthesis, back to the tree. When the chlorophyll dies in autumn, the carotene pigment in this MAPLE LEAF becomes visible. Carotene serves as an accessory pigment in photosynthesis, trapping solar energy and passing it to chlorophyll. The estimated length of the vein network in the leaves of even a single tree is staggering.

Carpet of Wood Anemones

Wood anemones, wind flowers, white stars
in the green firmament
of this Ayrshire copse,
thrown into panics by the wind's brute powers,
battered in the downpour's drops,
here in this moment of grace we find you,
each pale face turned upward
awaiting the insect's selfish kiss.

The WOOD ANEMONE is also known as the wind flower due to its frailty in the slightest breeze. *(Anemone is derived from the Greek anemos, wind.)* Each blossom turns to follow the sun round the sky, closing rapidly in dull weather.

Snawdraps

— for Duncan Glen

The blintert snawdrap can manage wi'oot
thae dowless flooers yirdit wi doot;
fir it can match Orion's pooers
richt throu the skinklin wee sma oors;
sae up it cams, an mebbe gies
thae laggard bauchles, bi degrees,
smeddum frae shame ti cam up tae
intil the air an the sin's ray;
but it's the yin that sterts the spring.
It sets the sin abune aa thing.

blintert: blown by boisterous gusty wind
dowless: feeble, lacking in strength or energy
yirdit: buried
skinklin: sparkling
bauchle: untidy or clumsy person
smeddum: spirit, energy, drive
sin: sun

The SNOWDROP is probably not native to
Britain. It may have been introduced from
central Europe in the Middle Ages.

Maidenhair Fern

Ayrshire

I spring from rock,
from the cleft in rock,
into light and space
in the face of the testing sea.
Where many would shrivel and die,
I know my chances and set
my spores, beget
my fronds of grace and green
from stone and calm tenacity.
I am the poetry of chlorophyll,
written on the page of rock
with the ink of water and light,
and the pen of unbending will.

MAIDENHAIR FERN. Fossil ferns 300 million
years old have been found. There are around
50 species in Britain, and they thrive mostly in
the west, where high rainfall suits them.

The Nature of Burns

It's not the rivers but the burns —
their unexpected dips and turns
like a poet's verse, inspired —
I like the most, chuckling alive
not gravid; shallow, mainly, and happy with it,
clean on their gravel beds, too quick
to suffer the reflection of a star.
Each with the happenstance of lyric,
like the burn at Candymill
punctuated by dippers,
that's never still
except in drought, lovely liquid syllables
weaving their sentence of life around the hill;
music
startling me into the world from my head, out
under the starry gossips.
Or this burn at Stronchullin
in Argyll, day and night
its flow of light and dark
through the glen of lichens and emerald mosses.
It's not the rivers but the burns ....
Where the sweetest water runs.
Where the spawning salmon go.

N.B. Candy Burn at Candymill
flows through the field below
Brownsbank Cottage.

STRONCHULLIN BURN, Argyll.

Dandelion Seeds

— for Aileen McIntyre

From somewhere —
 from the Pennines, from Skye,
will arrive the puff of air
 to make us fly.

In each barbed seed
 (as in a nib of gold)
though they call us weed
 is light untold —

to scatter like suns
 in the Cosmos's breath,
and billow long tons
 of blooms from death.

Barbs on the DANDELION's seed, clearly visible here, help it to cling on alighting, while the white 'feathers' act as parachutes. The flower's name derives from the French *dent de lion, lion's tooth*; its origin is unknown. Liver problems were once treated with a milky juice found in the dandelion's root.

Rosehip in Frost

— for Stewart Conn

Out below Orion now
    The old
 Jeweller of the night
Weds me with his diamonds;
 Yet, within my red
Storehouse of the dead
 Tomorrow sleeps,
   Petal and thorn
 For things unborn
Without thought for useless sorrow
    In the cold.

Vitamin C is one ingredient found in abundance in the hips of wild roses. Those collected through World War II produced the Vitamin C content of 25 million oranges. They made two and a half million bottles of rose hip syrup.

Crab Spider in Grass

In the minor infinities of green
the green crab spider won't be seen
by whatever will form its prey.
  Ignorant of place or date,
as if it were dead it rests in wait
for what may venture, soon or late,
  near, on this Easter day.
Mere yards away the people pass
on the chapel's path; and do not know
what rite is planned here, as they go,
in this stoneless church of grass.

Stealth and deception is the predatory ruse of this CRAB SPIDER in Argyll, probably *Misumena vatia*. It is often found camouflaged on wild flowers, where it captures insects seeking nectar. Size of spider: *c. 1cm.*

Face of Wolf Spider

Not from another planet but from this,
down among its underworld
the wolf-spider, black-headlamp-eyed,
fanged like the sabre-toothed tiger, prowls —
for creatures to despatch with its drugging kiss —
over its small savannahs and its plains.
I've seen its potential victims flee
in what appeared as terror
at the prospect of those pains.
The spider's not to blame. It didn't make its world.
I've seen it race in terror too
like Hector from Achilles, without a sound
when the spider-hunting *pompilid* wasp called round.

As well as being predators, WOLF SPIDERS — so called because they literally run down their prey — are preyed on by pompilid wasps, which sting them to paralyse them, then drag them to a nest and lay an egg nearby. The spider is thus still fresh when the egg hatches, and the grub eats the spider — literally — alive. This spider was in fact tiny, but is greatly magnified here. It measured just *1cm* across its legs.

Wood Sorrels

Here on the floor of the wood, not a puff
of air to distress our waiting calm,
we find waiting enough
as we bloom in our thousands,
a galaxy, our hearts open for the good
touch of the insect's tongue,
its specks of the finest gold. (Yes,
even in the gloom
of the wood is the dance
of sex.) The sea
trickles through the veins
of our petals, and the world's artificer
who sculpts out mountains
fashions us too in our delicacy,
to whom but the slightest breeze is a gale
sending us lashing and fluttering,
like crowds of girls holding onto their bonnets,
under the emerald of the spring birch trees.

WOOD SORREL is a common wild flower found in Scottish woods and on hedgebanks in May.

The Sundew's Speech

I skinkle here and wait
to be the insect's fate.
Admire if you will how light
turns my kind to a bright
galaxy of ruby and of green,
though it's not beauty that I mean
but the marriage of function and need.
Come, prey, let your clambering greed
find its end in my pinpoint glues —
I'll enfold you like a lover, use
your body's life, open and let
the wind blow your husk away, then set
in place again each fatal coronet.

SUNDEW is an insectivorous plant found in Scottish bogs. Growing on nitrogen-poor soil, it makes up for this by capturing insects on its glue-tipped leaves. *(Its white flower is small and insignificant.)* The leaf folds over and digests the insect's juices through its *stomata*, pores on the leaf surface. The leaf pictured here measured around *9mm* across.

Young Beech Leaves Emerging
in an Ayrshire Hedge

Inexorably, slowly,
flimsy at first
as silk with their silver fringes,
they push from within,
their miles of veins
of tenacious water
unfurling
them.

How the star-charged masses
from the packed caves,
innocuous armies of imperial May
roll
the stone
of winter
off!

Inexorable as love
that's heedless of what
convention allows,
their lime architecture
that gladdens the county,
their sunlight prisons
for winter's boughs.

YOUNG BEECH LEAVES: in May, beeches develop the slow lime haze which is the emergence of thousands and thousands of new leaves. Later, the leaves become a sombre green.

Dewdrops in Spider Web

Here is Proteus, the shape-changer,
who circles within you from head to foot
as blood,
lives in the jelly of the eye,
is at least two-thirds of you, and has
no problem abasing himself in mud
or flashing his fluent knives on the loch for miles
under the sun in space. Such disguises! —
fattener
of the autumn apple,
he gentles the flank of the salmon,
is a dull skinkler of the fields and lanes, under the winter moon.

Here is another —
a hundred eyes of dew
caught in the hammock web of a money spider
expecting flies.
Before the robbing sun arrives,
they gaze at themselves in you.

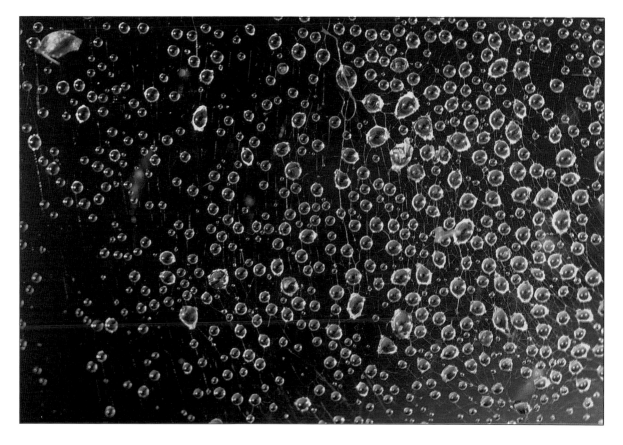

Dewdrops often gather around tiny droplets of 'glue' applied to the web by the spider during construction.

Chrysomelid Beetle Pollinating
Wild Orchid

This Chrysomelid beetle,
like a man in a pub,
only wanted a sweet sup
from the deep curved cup
of this Argyll orchid.
Nectar guides on her blossom's lips
will have guided him up
under the hood's pollinia
he must breach
to reach
the nectar.
And, as he did, he burst
a tiny bag of glue
at the base of those two
ingenious clubs of pollen
(each some three millimetres high)
and stuck them to his head,
where the drying of the glue
in theory should turn them down
to aim at the stigma of the next blossom
he drinks from, and dust it with pollen
for the orchid's fertilisation.
Poor little fellow,
like a man going out to the pub
who'd come home plastered
with lipstick, garter belt round his head—
had he home and wife to go to. Instead
he wanders in his stunning freedom,
weighted
with the little drum-torches —
that will light whole meadows
with orchids in season —
stuck to his head with glue.

The head of this BEETLE is
already weighted with pollinia —
small clubs of pollen — to fertilise
the orchid the insect is feeding
from.

Rock Pool

Twice a day the sea's tons roar
in again onto this rock pool —
four
beadlet anemones,
a whelk,
pale coralline —
opening the massive doors
and flooding with fresh brine
(as a brain is lit with an inspiration)
the small ground hollow in the rock.

Terrifying, exciting,
it must be for the pool's
jewel of clarity
stultified here,
to be scoured and swept
by the weighty
revelation
of the salty miles.

The creatures in this rock pool at Eilean Hoan, Sutherland are still covered by a few inches of sea-water. ANEMONES, out of water, become shapeless blobs, resembling jelly.

Gem Anemone

Under the sea
by day and night
the Gem Anemone,
which needs no light,
no bigger across than a fingernail,
stickily
captures the plankton.
While, in our peculiar air,
we multifariously
live, eat, sleep,
the Gem Anemone
attached to its constant rock
down there,
sways
in the tides
like a dancer,
mortal as us,
to its unheard music which can have no end.

This little ANEMONE, *Sagartia elegans,* var. *venusta,* was found at Barassie, Ayrshire. It's common in rock pools. I lit it up here like a spaceship to accentuate its tentacles. In life, it would measure around *12mm* across.

At Portencross

The Common Blenny or Shanny,
thick-lipped clown of the pool,
peering from cleft and cranny,
looks back skelly-eyed
when you gaze from above.
Twice a day his world is shaken
by the god who drowns the rock pool's brim,
by the swirl and swish and swash of the sluggish sea.
It cannot be love
as we know it that has him
guard the female's eggs
till they hatch and are coldly, saltily taken
and scattered,
yet I think him a chivalrous fish.

Blennius pholis, the COMMON BLENNY, is probably the commonest shore fish in Britain. The male guards the female's eggs, laid under stones, until they hatch. The fish grows to around *15cm* in length.

Hermit Crab

When you peer in like God to the rock pool,
at your shadow this crab —
nobody's fool — with a flick withdraws
into the home it lugs on its back.
Keep still. In a moment
the big right claw
shoves out, then the eyes on stalks,
as they clear the shell's ceiling, spring
up like levers, the long antennae
swish, the little sensors
between them
plink
like fingers, you'd think, upon
invisible piano keys.
Then it is out, like a clockwork toy,
traversing the floor of the rockpool,
home on its back, in perpetual crisis
as bloody old nature gave it a lack
of protection, unlike the rest of its family,
and it's a risky place, the sea.
At the sight of its trauchles the spirits lift,
its shell invention under stress,
its nakedness like some creative gift:
comic, with a serious end —
this permanent refugee
from danger's
country.

Experiments using shells made of glass show that the HERMIT CRAB grips the inside of the shell with appendages on its soft abdomen; as it grows, it frequently has to change to a larger shell, a dangerous proceeding, marked by great care and nervousness on the crab's part. This specimen measured some $3\,cm$ across.

Dahlia Sea Anemone

You'll barely understand
this world, up in your air

so light and far and wide and clear that turns
me when hoisted up to a shapeless blob,

vulnerable and bare,
under the downdrag of gravity.

The sea's my joy: the great weight of the sea —
stretching from here to America —

pulled by the moon, swills over me, feeds me,
grants me symmetrical beauty. I sway

in its vast surges of power,
I wait for food I can sting and fold

to my mouth with my many arms,
the petals of my death-flower.

Below me in the stretching deeps
are denizens of the sea, and above

through the brilliant element clear to space,
you creatures far stranger than me

walk upright, all of us serving the unknown aim
of what made us from nothing and has no name.

Britain's largest rock pool and shallow water sea anemone, the DAHLIA captures prey using stinging cells in the tentacles. The central vent functions both as its mouth and its anus. This specimen was around *14cm* across its tentacles.

Shore Crab

Haw, Jimmy, dinnae mess wi me.
Fancy yer chances, eh? Eh? We'll see.
Naw, they dinnae caw
me Shug the Claw
fer naethin. Mon, square go then. Srang,
ye feart? Ahve taen a haill gang
o the likes o ye at wance.
Dinnae reckon yer chance
noo, eh? When ye get tae hell
ah'll be waitin there fer ye. Caw
me a scroonger, eh? Aye, awa
an rin ti yer maw
ya wimp! Mind o Shug the Claw.

The SHORE CRAB, *Carcinus maenas,* is common in rock pools, and measures up to *14cm* across. It is primarily a scavenger and an omnivore.

Young Vole Running Up a Branch

One mistake—
he's done
for, nature being no
forgiving mother.

Look — he's in mid-
step, the paw
poised between
alighting upon

the law that leads
to death and the law
that means life
pittering on.

VOLES are preyed on by owls, foxes, badgers, weasels and stoats. They rarely live long.

Green-Veined White Butterfly
Caught on Sundew

The butterfly's kirkyard is the sundew's meadow,
the falcon's joy is the field vole's shadow.
Thyme grows over the rabbit's skull,
the duckling is flight to the black-backit gull.
Change, change, mean all the many
mouths, each as good as any.
Birth, consumption, mating, death, and birth
make up the song of ancient Earth.

GREEN-VEINED WHITE caught on SUNDEW:
the insectivorous plant Sundew, *Drosera
rotundifolia,* the gummy leaves of which are
visible here to the right, usually catches
smaller insects *(see page 97).* Within a few
square feet of bog at Shewalton Moss,
Ayrshire, however, the author found half a
dozen butterflies trapped in this way — each a
meal possibly too substantial for the plant to
digest. Actual size of butterfly: *4cm.*

Some other books published by **LUATH** PRESS

NATURAL SCOTLAND

Wild Scotland

James McCarthy

Photographs by Laurie Campbell. Foreword by Magnus Magnusson

ISBN 0 946487 37 5 £7.50 PBK

The essential site by site guide to the best of natural Scotland.

The Highland Geology Trail

John L Roberts

ISBN 0 946487 36 7 £4.99 PBK

New edition of the highly regarded guide to the amazing geology of the highlands.

'*...a lucid introduction to the geological record in general, a jargon-free exposition of the regional background, and a series of descriptions of specific localities of geological interest on a "trail" around the highlands.*
John Roberts has created a resource of great value which is eminently usable by anyone with an interest in the outdoors... the best bargain you are likely to get as a geology book in the foreseeable future.'
JIM JOHNSTON, *Press and Journal*

Scotland, Land and People: An Inhabited Solitude

James McCarthy

ISBN 0 946487 57 X £7.99 PBK

'*Scotland is the country above all others that I have seen, in which a man of imagination may carve out his own pleasures; there are so many inhabited solitudes.*'
DOROTHY WORDSWORTH, in her journal of August 1803.

An informed and thought provoking profile of Scotland's unique landscapes and the impact of humans on what we see now and in the future.

Rum: Nature's Island

Magnus Magnusson

ISBN 0 946487 32 4 £7.95 PBK

The fascinating story of a Hebridean island from the earliest times through to the Clearances and its period as the sporting playground of a Lancashire industrial magnate, and on to its rebirth as a National Nature Reserve, a model for the active ecological management of Scotland's wild places.

Luath Press Limited

committed to publishing well written books worth reading

LUATH PRESS takes its name from Robert Burns, whose little collie Luath (*Gael.*, swift or nimble) tripped up Jean Armour at a wedding and gave him the chance to speak to the woman who was to be his wife and the abiding love of his life. Burns called one of *The Twa Dogs* Luath after Cuchullin's hunting dog in *Ossian's Fingal.* Luath Press grew up in the heart of Burns country, and now resides a few steps up the road from Burns' first lodgings on Edinburgh's Royal Mile.

Luath offers you distinctive writing with a hint of unexpected pleasures.

Luath Press Limited
543/2 Castlehill
The Royal Mile
Edinburgh EH1 2ND
Telephone: 0131 225 4326 (*24 HOURS*)
Fax: 0131 225 4324
email: gavin.macdougall@luath.co.uk
Website: www.luath.co.uk